Gathered and Sent

Gathered and Sent

AN INTRODUCTION TO WORSHIP

PARTICIPANT BOOK

By Karen G. Bockelman

Art by Nicholas T. Markell

Augsburg Fortress

GATHERED AND SENT
An Introduction to Worship
Participant Book

This participant book has a corresponding leader guide.

Scripture quotations, unless otherwise noted, are from the New Revised Standard Version Bible © 1989 Division of Christian Education of the National Council of the Churches of Christ in the United States of America. Used by permission.

Prayers and liturgical texts acknowledged as *LBW* are copyright © 1978 *Lutheran Book of Worship* and those acknowledged as *With One Voice* are copyright © 1995 Augsburg Fortress.

Other quoted materials are acknowledged on page 61.

Book Design: Ellen Maly
Editors: Dennis Bushkofsky, Lynn Joyce Hunter, and Rebecca Lowe

Manufactured in the U.S.A.

ISBN 0-8066-3844-3   3-4157

03   2   3   4   5

Table of Contents

CHAPTER ONE: GOD 6

CHAPTER TWO: GATHERING 14

CHAPTER THREE: WORD 24

CHAPTER FOUR: BATH 32

CHAPTER FIVE: MEAL 42

CHAPTER SIX: SENDING 50

APPENDIX: SEASONS AND FESTIVALS 59

ACKNOWLEDGMENTS 61

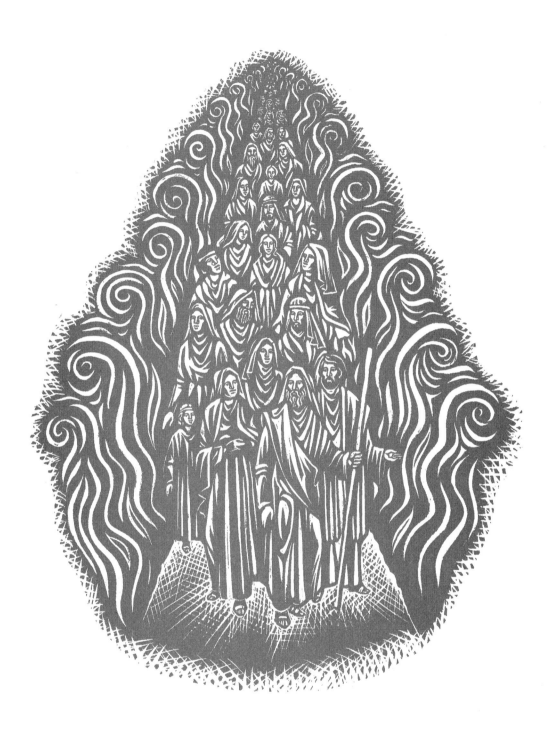

God

It all begins with God—creation, life, beauty, truth, service, joy, hope. Worship, too, begins with God. Certainly God has commanded worship, but even more at the heart of worship is the story of God's desire to love God's created world into abundant life. Worship is where we meet that God—the God who created the heavens and the earth, the God who loved and wooed a stubborn and defiant people, the God who "became flesh and lived among us . . . full of grace and truth" (John 1:14). Worship is not so much a place as it is an event, an encounter with the living God.

Human beings are curious about God. Children, especially, can drive parents nearly crazy with their impossible-to-answer questions about everything, including God. At the age of five our daughter asked regularly and insistently, "Where was God born? Where did God come from?" No answer would satisfy her, especially no answer that tried to explain that God did not come from anywhere, God has always been and will always be. Finally, in desperation, we answered, "Australia!"

As I look back on it, I think she was not so much asking for God's birthplace as for the assurance that there was somewhere she could count on finding God. It is hard for all of us, not just for five-year-olds, to grasp a God we cannot seem to see, hear, or touch. Faith can go only so far! Now that our daughter is older, she continues to ask about the presence of God. "How do I know God is real? How do I know God is really there?"

Since everything we possess, and everything in heaven and on earth besides, is daily given and sustained by God, it inevitably follows that we are in duty bound to love, praise, and thank [God] without ceasing.

THE LARGE CATECHISM

❧ FINDING GOD

Our daughter's questions about finding God have moved from space to time. We talk not so much about where to find God as when to find God. We have begun to speak of God being present when we pray. We include family and friends in our prayers. We pray for soccer games and lost animals. We pray for those who are sad and for those who are joyful. We pray for our nation and for the world. We have our devotions at bedtime to ask God to be with us through the night. We also pray at mealtimes.

Again the questions come. "If God knows everything, doesn't God already know who's sick? If God gives us our food, why do we need to pray about it?" Our prayers don't tell God anything God doesn't already know. Our prayers do remind us that God watches over everything and everyone. They serve as a reminder of God's presence in our lives.

We all need regular reminders of God's presence. For many, personal and family prayer takes on certain patterns. Morning prayer starts the day with the reminder that each day is God's. Prayers at noon place our daily activities of work, school, and leisure squarely in God's sight. Evening prayer assures us that God "will neither slumber nor sleep" (Ps. 121:4), keeping watch over us through the night. Prayers before travel put our safety into God's hands. Prayers at mealtime keep us mindful of God's gifts and our calling to share with those in need.

But personal and family prayer is not enough. We need a larger community to sustain us when we grow lazy or careless. And so I find myself speaking much more often of God's presence in the worshiping community. Worship is where we can count on receiving the gifts of God. There we will hear God's words, and we will eat, drink, taste, smell, and touch God in bread, wine, and water. In gathering, word, bath, meal, and sending, God comes to each of us.

❧ DUTY AND DELIGHT

"It is our duty and delight at all times and in all places to give thanks to you O Lord . . ." *(Contemporary Worship 2*, The Holy Communion). Worship is our duty. "Praise the Lord," commands the psalmist.

"Pray without ceasing," demands Paul. "In our family we do not skip church," declares Mom. Sometimes we settle for duty. It is what's expected. It is part of the routine. Even if it is boring, even if it is long, even if we are just going through the motions, even if we are angry, even if we are not fully present, we go to worship. Worship is a discipline God uses to shape us for service in the world and for life in the kingdom. We thank and praise God, even when we don't feel like it, only to discover in the doing that God is the source of our joy.

In worship duty and delight flow in and out of one another. We discover the delight God takes in all of creation and the love God has for us. We learn to enjoy God, to rejoice in God's gifts, to find delight in the service God has given us to do. Praise is what human beings do when we speak of what or who we care about most deeply. What we honor, respect, and adore is what we worship. It is our duty and delight to give worship to God.

WHAT GOD?

Worship begins with God, but the question is: what god? Whom or what do you regard with respect, honor, or devotion? To whom or what does your heart cling? Of whom or what do you stand in awe? Where do you place your trust? To whom or what do you look for all good? In whom or what do you find refuge in every time of need? How you answer those questions identifies your god.

The Ten Commandments begin with the identity of God. "I am the LORD your God, who brought you out of the land of Egypt, out of the house of slavery; you shall have no other gods before me" (Exod. 20:2-3). This is no laughing matter with God. If we are to have a god, one whom we honor above anything else, it is to be the true God, one who is worthy of our fear, love, and trust.

❧ IMAGE AND WORSHIP

Of course we do not have God, if "having" means that we possess God. But we do have images of God. There are pictures, stories, metaphors, glimpses of God, especially in the Bible, that speak to each of us heart to heart. God is rock, woman in labor, friend, warrior, ruler of the universe, judge, creator, destroyer, lover, servant, father, shepherd . . . these images are not just from the Bible, but are shaped by culture and experience. No one image can encompass God, but it can point to the God who is beyond.

Our images of God shape our worship. The college where I served as campus pastor has a building which serves as both performing arts center and chapel. The main hall is wide and shallow, keeping as short a distance as possible between the performers and the audience. For one special occasion we attempted to create a formal, cathedral-like worship space. A huge banner depicting a cross-shaped human figure was hung on the wall facing the seating area. The altar was placed at the top of a high platform against the banner wall. Many stairs led to the altar area. The pulpit was similarly elevated. A processional cross and large, torch-like candles were arranged in formal balance. The space looked very different from its usual worship arrangement.

Some time before the service was to begin, a student usher wandered rather casually through the doors to receive his instructions. Halfway down the aisle he stopped suddenly, his eyes growing wider and wider as they traveled upward. "Now," he murmured, *"this* is a *church!"* Something about the space—its formality, its illusion of height and distance—matched his image of God, opening the way for a worship experience that touched him at the deepest level.

That same worship arrangement would not be a comfortable place in which to encounter God in the image of friend or lover. Someone who says, "I can worship God on the golf course or at the lake" may not be justifying absence from church as much as saying that worshiping God the creator requires the presence of nature. Someone else who longs for the stillness of God in the midst of a chaotic world may cherish silence in worship. One who longs for God to break through the isolation and loneliness of life may seek energy and exuberance, especially in music. We are drawn to worship experiences that connect with our images of God, but we also need the images of those around us.

No one can ever fully imagine God, because God is always more and always other. A god we human beings could fully know would not be God. Worship is never only one experience but many. Any worship shaped by an image of God is also challenged by God's surprise. Just when I long for cozy conversation with a friend, God speaks to me in a voice of thunder, out of a cloud of fire and smoke. Just when I fall on my knees, trembling in the presence of the Almighty, God invites me for a walk in the garden. Just when I cling to the formal rules of protocol, all structure and distance, God sweeps me into a laughing dance.

COMMUNITY

Worship belongs not only to God—but to the community of believers. Worship is shaped in the gathered community with its many members, many images, many needs, and many gifts. We are present in worship as living reminders for one another. We are reminders of the richness of God. We are reminders of the duty and the delight. We can never quite predict which words, gestures, music, actions, faces, or voices will call us to our faithful duty or our deep delight.

It is no easy task to be a worshiping community. We are not a gathering of like-minded folks, each singing the same song in the same way. We are much more like Jesus' own ragged band of disciples, wildly diverse in personality, attitude, and need. In worship we seek a unity greater than the sum of ourselves, but we are not always sure how to go about it. Almost recklessly we let loose with song and speech, ceremony and gesture, silence and activity, and by the grace of God, something we call worship comes of it.

Still, not just anything goes. Worship begins with God and so it must speak truthfully of God. Worship is our constant duty and delight, and so it needs to be repeated. Worship happens in community, and so it develops rhythm, form, and shape. Worship is a public event, and so it must speak truthfully about the world. Worship is open to newcomers and strangers, and so it is approached with purpose and intentionality. Worship takes the form of ritual, a repeated pattern. This is true if there are printed worship books or not, if prayers are written out or spoken freely, if the scripture readings are assigned or chosen, if the building was designed as a church or a gymnasium or a store front. It is not a matter of ritual or no ritual, but rather of *what* ritual.

Another word for ritual is *pattern*. Christian worship has been shaped by the practice of Israel, the New Testament, the writings of the early church, and the experience and documents of various Christian denominations. From the earliest days of the church, Christian worship has been marked by a pattern of gathering, word, meal, and sending.

One of the earliest descriptions of Christian worship sounds surprisingly contemporary.

> On Sunday all are gathered together in unity. The records of the apostles or the writings of the prophets are read for as long as time allows. The presider exhorts and invites us into the pattern of these good things. Then we all stand and offer prayer.

> When we have concluded the prayer, bread is set out together with wine. . . . The presider then offers prayer and thanksgiving and the people sing out their assent, saying the "Amen." There is a distribution of the things over which thanks has been said and each person participates, and these things are sent to those who are not present.

> Those who are prosperous give what they wish according to each one's own choice, and the collection is deposited with the presider, who aids orphans and widows, those in want because of disease, those in prison, and foreigners who are staying here.

> We hold this meeting together on Sunday since it is the first day, on which God, having transformed darkness and matter, created the world. On the same day Jesus Christ our Savior rose from the dead. On Sunday

he appeared to his apostles and disciples and taught them these things which we present to you ("The Apology of Justin Martyr (c. 150 A.D.)," in *With One Voice*, p. 6).

This ancient yet contemporary pattern teaches us the essentials of Christian worship: The people of God gather in community. They hear God's word read in the scriptures and proclaimed in preaching. They pray for the needs of the world and for the church's mission, receiving an offering for the support of that mission and the concrete needs of others. The community receives Christ in the bread and wine of communion, and is strengthened for a life of witness and service in the world. The community welcomes newcomers in baptism.

This is the worship pattern that we will explore in the coming chapters.

QUESTIONS FOR REFLECTION

In the worlds where you live, work, or play, who or what asks for or demands your fear, love, and trust?

When you close your eyes in prayer, how do you imagine the God to whom you pray? When has an unexpected or surprising image of God appeared in your mind's eye? What was that image?

What do you think of as a duty? As a delight?

What repeated patterns give shape to your day?

CHAPTER TWO

Gathering

Gathering is the name given to the first part of our corporate worship. The word *gathering* conveys a sense of both verb and noun. Gathering is what believers do and it describes who they are; gathering is also what God does. From the very beginning of the church, believers have gathered, have come together. The description of the Pentecost event that is remembered as the birthday of the church begins, "When the day of Pentecost had come, they were all together in one place" (Acts 2:1). Justin Martyr's second-century description of Christian worship begins, "On Sunday all are gathered together in unity."

Now, many centuries later, believers come together physically in one place. Much of this gathering is informal and somewhat spontaneous. The single mom and her kids, the retired couple, parents and children, teenagers and singles all make their way to the place of worship. So too does the pastor, the custodian, musicians, readers, teachers, and greeters. Some come alone, some as families or with groups of friends; first a few, then more.

There is a Lutheran college which formalizes the act of gathering on the first Sunday of every school year. On that morning, a procession leaves from the campus chapel and winds its way past all the residence halls, picking up students as it goes. In this way the worshiping community is gathered and led back to the worship center. Although the tradition began when there was no chapel on campus and students gathered to walk to church in town, it continues in large part because of its power to mold and shape a community.

For where two or three are gathered in my name, I am there among them.

MATTHEW 18:20

We also gather, bringing ourselves with us—our hopes and fears, our needs and gifts, our sorrows and joys. Some of us are deliberate in our gathering, some are frantic, some reluctant, some eager. We come from a variety of experiences, in different moods, with differing expectations. We come as ourselves, but not to forget or escape or lose ourselves in the crowd. We do not check ourselves at the church door in exchange for a "one-size-fits-all-believers" identity. Worship is whenever and wherever we place ourselves in the hands of God. It is the time and place when we entrust our realities to God in the presence and with the support of those who join us in the gathering.

Worship is the experience that brings us together in all our individual diversity and shapes us into the one body of Christ. In many congregations music plays an important role both in gathering people together and in giving them an identity. Just as music can bring together many instruments and voices for a common purpose, so can it gather the thoughts and hearts of a diverse assembly to focus on its common purpose.

✠ CALLED OUT

God is the one who calls us from the scattered places of our daily lives into the gathering we call the church. The word *church* comes from the Greek word *ecclesia*, which literally means those who are "called out." In other words, to be the church is not just to come together, but to be "the gathering" in the world. While gathering for worship starts with the act of going to church, it is more truthfully the act of becoming the church.

> I believe that by my own understanding or strength I cannot believe in Jesus Christ my Lord or come to him, but instead the Holy Spirit has called me through the gospel, enlightened me with his gifts, made me holy, and kept me in the true faith, just as he calls, gathers, enlightens, and makes holy the whole Christian church on earth and keeps it with Jesus Christ in the one common, true faith (Wengert 1994).

✠ THE PEOPLE'S WORK

Those who gather for worship are the baptized children of God, sisters and brothers of Jesus Christ and of one another. We are members of the church, citizens of God's realm. As citizens we have work to do. *Liturgy*, the word we use for the order of worship, also comes from a Greek word, one that originates in the arena of politics rather than that of religion. It speaks of civic responsibility, participation by all in order to serve the common good. In a world where many prefer to sit back and be entertained, those who gather for worship are people at work.

There is a variety of work to be done in worship. There is need of preaching and presiding—reading scripture, leading prayer, distributing communion, providing music. There is work of hospitality—welcoming all who gather, giving directions, providing refreshments. Some work is done behind the scenes— there are lights to be turned on, windows to be washed, rest rooms to be cleaned.

Perhaps the least thought about but very important work is that done by each member of the worshiping assembly. It is work to listen to scripture and to relate our own lives to it. It is work to confess our sins and to receive forgiveness. It is work to give voice to the needs of the world and to discern what God calls us to do about those needs. All baptized persons are called upon to sing, attend to God's word, give testimony to their faith, pray, offer gifts, welcome newcomers, receive communion, be blessed, and be sent forth to serve.

There is room in the gathering for those who are not yet citizens. Guests, onlookers, those exploring membership, and even the just-plain-curious find their ways into the gathering. When they do, they will see not just a room full of individuals, but the working body of Christ. They may not understand all the tasks. Not everything they see or experience will make sense. On the surface, worship may not look like what they want. At its best, however, seekers will find in the gathering a sense that lives are changed by the presence of Christ.

℘ SUNDAYS AND SEASONS

God's people gather in rhythms of weeks, seasons, and festivals. In our culture we keep the calendar year from January 1 through December 31, but we live by many, often competing calendars. The school calendar begins in September. The fiscal year seems to start on the first of almost any month but January. We speak of sports seasons and of fashion seasons. Different faiths keep different religious calendars. All of these calendar rhythms have some power to shape us.

The Jewish theologian Abraham Joshua Heschel relates a story illustrating the power of such rhythms.

> Once a rabbi was immured by his persecutors in a cave, where not a ray of light could reach him, so that he knew not when it was day or when it was night. Nothing tormented him so much as the thought that he was now hindered from celebrating the Sabbath with song and prayer, as he had been wont to do from his youth. Beside this an almost unconquerable desire to smoke caused him much pain. He worried and reproached himself that he could not conquer this passion. All at once, he perceived that it suddenly vanished; a voice said within him: "Now it is Friday evening! for this was always the hour when my longing for that which is forbidden on the Sabbath regularly left me." Joyfully he rose up and with loud voice thanked God and blessed the Sabbath day. So it went on from week to week; his tormenting desire for tobacco regularly vanished at the incoming of each Sabbath (Heschel 1951).

Sunday is the cornerstone of the Christian calendar. It is the primary day on which we gather to worship, the original feast day. Sunday is the first day of the week, the day identified in scripture as the day on which Christ rose from the dead (Matt. 28:1; Mark 16:2; Luke 24:1; John 20:1). Sunday is also the day the risen Christ first appeared (Mark 16:9; John 20:19). Sunday is the "Lord's day"; each one a "little Easter." When the earliest Christians gathered for worship, Sunday was still a working day. Sunday worship was not designed to take advantage of a day off work but to bear witness to Christ, his resurrection, and the hope of his return.

The first day of the week is also remembered as the first day of creation, the day when God transformed darkness into light. And, in our calendar's marking of a seven-day week, Sunday can be counted as the *eighth* day—the day which follows *and* begins each week. It symbolizes the beginning of the world as well as the world's last day.

All other days grow out of and toward Sunday. Worship on Sunday proclaims Christ as the center of time.

The shape of Sunday worship is the service of word and sacrament. The proclamation of the word of God and the celebration of communion are intimately connected. In both we encounter Jesus Christ, the living Word of God. The order of our liturgy has been used by generations of Christians. We gather in God's presence, hear God's word, baptize and remember baptism, share in the Lord's supper, receive God's blessing, and are sent out in mission to the world.

Of course, Sunday is not the only day when it is appropriate for worship. No day should end without prayer and praise of God, whether in the home or in a gathering of Christians. Daily prayer, personal or family devotions, the celebration of local or national festivals, and important life occasions such as weddings or funerals are all occasions for worship. These events are markers along the way, carrying us from Sunday to Sunday, keeping us centered on Christ in the community.

The rhythm of the church year is not just a weekly rhythm. Christians also follow a yearly calendar of festivals like Christmas, Epiphany, Easter, and Pentecost (see appendix). Surrounding these festivals are seasons of focus and emphasis that lead to and flow from them. The church year begins with Advent, a time of anticipating the coming of Christ both in the birth at Bethlehem and in a future coming. It is a season of preparation. The Epiphany season is a time of revelation, a bridge between the birth of Jesus and his suffering. Lent is another season of preparation, forty days of focus on rebirth and renewal as we get ready to celebrate Easter, the chief festival of the year. Our preparations intensify during the three days immediately preceding Easter when the drama of the salvation story is brought into our own experience. Although we tend to think of Easter as Easter Sunday (one great festival day), in the church year it lasts for seven weeks—one extended feast. The fifty days of Easter rejoicing culminate in the day of Pentecost when the risen Christ sends the Spirit to the church. The long stretch between Pentecost and the next Advent is often called "the time of the church." The focus is less on the events of Jesus' life than on the church's growth in mission and service as it reflects on the ministry and teachings of Jesus.

Still another calendar for Christians is the cycle of lesser festivals, commemorations, and special occasions. This calendar celebrates the lives of the saints, both from biblical and later times, as well as observing anniversaries, national holidays, and emphases such as peace or Christian unity. While few congregations have a worship schedule that can make use of the whole list of commemorations, most could celebrate at least some of these days.

One of the great joys in living with the church's calendar is its richness in mood and focus. Just as God cannot be fully understood through any one image, the story of God's relationship with God's people cannot be captured in any one mood. Some seasons are reflective, some celebratory. Some days call us to pay particular attention to issues of social justice, while others point us to mystics and artists. On some occasions we focus on our own needs and heritage; on others we rejoice in the rich diversity of the whole people of God.

Sometimes, and at some places, the church year and the secular calendar fit together well. In the Northern Hemisphere the days begin to get longer just as the church, in Epiphany, celebrates Jesus Christ as the light of the world. Easter's celebration of rebirth and new life comes as that same part of the world moves into spring. At other times the church calendar runs counter to that of the world. The most often noted of these countercultural times is Advent, when the church is still waiting and hoping for the coming of Christ while the shopping malls are filled with the sights, sounds, and sales of Christmas.

Whatever the fit or misfit of the church's calendar with the many calendars of the world, we use it to make an orderly witness to Christ in time. We clothe the skeletons of our calendar with changes in the environment and art of our worship space, as well as variety in words and music. Colors change from blue to white to purple to gold to red to green. Textures can be smooth as silk or rough as homespun.

There are times of few words and plain, simple music, as well as times when we "pull out all the stops." The full richness of human creativity is used in the service of proclaiming Christ to the world.

SETTING THE TONE

The opening part of our liturgy, the part we title "gathering," is far more than just a practical way of getting everyone in their places before the worship service begins. Gathering is itself worship. God calls us from the world to a new place, a place of acceptance and community. In the gathering we have contact with other believers. In the gathering we shape a common life of faith. In the gathering we are welcomed in Jesus' name and we welcome others. We sing and we pray. We place ourselves in the hand of God and imagine the future.

Long ago the prophet Isaiah encouraged a scattered people with a vision of their return to Jerusalem and of a gathering of all nations, drawn to God's glory.

> Nations shall come to your light,
>   and kings to the brightness of your dawn.
> Lift up your eyes and look around;
>   they all gather together, they come to you;
> your sons shall come from far away,
>   and your daughters shall be carried on their nurses' arms.
> Then you shall see and be radiant;
>   your heart shall thrill and rejoice . . .
>
> (Isa. 60:3-5a)

In Revelation, John describes a vision of a final gathering of all God's people, drawn into God's presence in the new Jerusalem, where they will worship God forever and ever.

> Then I saw a new heaven and a new earth . . . I saw the holy city, the new Jerusalem, coming down out of heaven from God. . . . I saw no temple in the city, for its temple is the Lord God the Almighty and the Lamb. And the city has no need of sun or moon to shine on it, for the glory of God is its light, and its lamp is the Lamb. The nations will walk by its light, and

the kings of the earth will bring their glory into it. Its gates will never be shut by day—and there will be no night there. People will bring into it the glory and the honor of the nations (Rev. 21:1-2, 22-26).

Every gathering for worship, however large or small, is in some way a preview of what is yet to come.

QUESTIONS FOR REFLECTION

Remember the last time you went to church. What did you bring with you—what experiences, what mood, what expectations?

What do you really like about the way you and the rest of your congregation come together for worship? What bothers you?

What "work" do you do in worship?

What are the calendars you live by? How does the church's calendar fit in? or not?

CHAPTER THREE

ᚠ ᚠ ᚠ ᚠ ᚠ

Word

God's people have come together—from home and work-place, alone or with friends or family, in many moods, from many experiences, with many expectations. In this time of gathering we find a common identity as the body of Christ. We become aware of one another and of God, in whose presence we stand. We collect our thoughts in prayer and turn attentively to the word of God.

But haven't we already heard words? Our Sunday morning worship is full of them—old words and new words, strange words and famil-iar words, obscure words and in-house words. Whatever the words, there are lots of them—one after another. It may seem, at times, that the words pile up like leaves in fall—an extravagance of words for the worship leader or preacher to play with. What is different about this section of our worship, entitled "word"?

During a long-ago visit to my then three-year-old nephew, he invited me to play church. "You sit there," he said, pointing to a spot on the floor in front of him. He stood up, tall and straight, and opened a book. Solemnly he spoke, "God, God, God, God, God." Each word was punctuated by a slight, sharp nod of his head. "God, God, God," he paused to turn the page, "God, God, God, God, God." "Now," he instructed me, "you say Amen."

Clearly my nephew associated church with words—serious words, read or spoken by a leader and affirmed by the congregation. He also knew, just as clearly, that all the words, heard and spoken, were, at their heart, one word: God. The many words of worship proclaim

The word of the Lord.
Thanks be to God.

_____

WITH ONE VOICE

God. What's more, these words are not just words about God, but the word *of* God, the word God speaks to us.

℘ GOD'S SPEECH

In the Bible there is a close connection between word and event, especially God's words. God's words are powerful. When God speaks things happen. God created the world by speaking it into being. "Then God said, 'Let there be light'; and there was light" (Gen. 1:3). In even more vivid language the prophet Isaiah describes the power of God's speech.

> For as the rain and the snow come down from heaven,
>   and do not return there until they have watered the earth,
> making it bring forth and sprout,
>   giving seed to the sower and bread to the eater,
> so shall my word be that goes out from my mouth;
> it shall not return to me empty,
> but it shall accomplish that which I purpose,
>   and succeed in the thing for which I sent it.
>
> (Isa. 55:10-11)

In the Hebrew language of the Old Testament, the same term can be used for both *word* and for a significant or meaningful event. God communicates not just verbally—by putting thoughts in the mind—but by doing significant things in human lives and history. God's rescue of the Israelites from slavery in Egypt spoke of freedom and promise.

In this same way, Christians have understood Jesus as God's Word. Jesus' birth, death, and resurrection in first-century Palestine was a significant, meaningful event. Jesus not only spoke in God's name, but was God's own speech made human. "And the Word became flesh and lived among us, and we have seen his glory, the glory as of a father's only son, full of grace and truth" (John 1:14). Jesus is God's living Word.

℘ WORD AND WORDS

It may seem strange to think of a person, Jesus, as Word. When we talk about the word of God we are more likely to think of a book, the words of the Bible. For my nephew, playing church required "reading" words from a book. But the words of scripture are the word of God precisely because they record the word-events through which God has spoken to humankind.

The words of the Old Testament—the stories, the songs, the proverbs, and the prophecies—remind us where we have come from and how God has sustained us throughout history. The words of the gospels tell the good news of God's saving Word, Jesus Christ. The letters (epistles) of the New Testament are words of guidance as Christians seek to live in the world. Over time the church has settled on the words of the Old and New Testaments as being the written word of God.

God did not finish speaking to us when the ink dried on the last book of the Bible. God still acts and speaks in the world, but does so in ways that can be easily overlooked. We can recognize God's present speech in the world only in light of how God has spoken in the past. When we hear again the story of Israel, and especially when we remember God's presence and activity in Jesus Christ, we are able to understand how God continues to speak to us.

PROCLAIMING THE WORD

Every Sunday God speaks to us through the word. In this speaking we are brought face to face not only with God, but also with ourselves. The word is a mirror in which we see ourselves as we really are. Through the word we are led to a relationship with God, not just to knowledge about God.

The heart of what we call the liturgy of the word is the public reading of scripture and its interpretation through preaching, song, and prayer. This part of our worship has its roots in the Jewish synagogue tradition. While in exile, Israel kept its identity by recalling what God had done, rejoicing in that history, and thanking God for it. Justin Martyr's description of early Christian worship contains the same elements: "The records of the apostles or the writings of the prophets are read for as long as time allows. The presider exhorts and invites us into the pattern of these good things. Then we all stand and offer prayer."

Proclamation of God's word is not just something to be done by pastors or preachers. All the baptized share responsibility for speaking and teaching God's good news. In the worship service, lay people (that is, not pastors) serve as assisting ministers, sharing in the reading of scripture and in leading the prayers. The whole congregation sings hymns and speaks words which proclaim the word of God. Music, the visual arts, and even the environment of our worship spaces embody God's word.

There are rhythms to this shared proclamation—rhythms of reading and singing, of speech and silence, of one voice and many. God's word is read; the congregation responds in song. Silence after the readings or the sermon allows time for the words to sink in and the word to be taken to heart. The creed and the prayers allow those who are gathered to say "yes" to the word they have heard and to entrust to God's mercy the needs of the world.

WHAT IS READ?

If the Bible is God's written word, you might expect that the whole Bible would be read, over time, in worship. More than once in my life I have determined to read the Bible from cover to cover. I usually start out pretty well—Genesis contains some pretty exciting stuff. But somewhere around Leviticus or Numbers I get bogged down. Let's face it, there are some parts that are more interesting, more moving, more accessible, more helpful, more suitable for public reading and commentary than others.

Since the early Middle Ages, the church has provided a *lectionary*, a list of readings for Sunday worship, to assist pastors and congregations in their public reading of the scriptures and to connect those readings to the church year. The texts chosen are not arbitrary; they are not dictated by the whim or taste of an individual. They represent years of accumulated wisdom on the part of the ecumenical church. Above all, the readings chosen for the lectionary provide a careful, comprehensive, systematic, and faithful way of keeping worship centered on the life, death, and resurrection of Jesus Christ. Much of the church (Methodist, Presbyterian, Reformed, Roman Catholic, United

Church of Christ, Disciples of Christ, Episcopal, Lutheran) now uses the same or a very similar three-year cycle of readings.

Lectionaries such as the *Revised Common Lectionary* or that of *Lutheran Book of Worship* provide three readings (from the Old Testament, the New Testament letters, and the gospels) and a psalm for every Sunday and festival. The Gospel of John is read at major festivals, and in each of three consecutive years the gospel readings are taken largely from Matthew, then Mark, and then Luke. The *Revised Common Lectionary* provides two sets of Old Testament readings after Pentecost; one set complements the gospel, the other features sequential readings from various Old Testament books. During the festival half of the church year (Advent through the day of Pentecost), the second reading complements the gospel. In the second half of the year, selections from the epistles are read in consecutive order.

Why not let preachers or worship leaders choose their own texts? While that might be interesting for a while, over the long run such a practice would all too quickly narrow the proclamation of the word. Using an approved lectionary keeps a congregation in touch with the ecumenical church. It ensures that a broader selection of scripture will be read and heard. The interplay of three readings is a reminder that the Bible does not give easy, simple answers to human questions. The preacher is often forced by those readings to wrestle with uncomfortable truths about humanity, about the world, and about God. Above all, the lectionary guides the preacher in the task of "showing forth Christ."

WHAT IS PREACHED?

There are two common misconceptions about sermons. One is that there is a "lectionary" of sermons—an assigned set of sermons, a book somewhere, from which pastors get their words. The other is that pastors don't need to "prepare" sermons; they just stand up on

Sunday morning and talk about what's going on in the world and the church. Martin Luther insisted that the preacher's primary task is to proclaim the gospel—that is, to "show forth Christ." Such preaching is not easy; it must be rooted in scripture and speak to a particular group of people in a concrete place and time. The most learned analysis of scripture is not a proclamation of God's word if it does not make Christ known to the people present. The most interesting, intriguing, and even moving speeches in the world are not proclamation of God's word if they do not serve an encounter with the living Christ. The preacher needs to know both the Bible and the world.

The sermon is not a time to lecture, impress, or entertain the congregation. Just being good with words doesn't mean the word is proclaimed. The sermon is the time to point as clearly and directly as possible to Jesus Christ, inviting all who are present to live out that word in their daily lives.

WHAT IS SUNG?

The liturgy of the word includes three primary responses that are often sung by the worshiping assembly. The psalm follows the first reading, often continuing a theme introduced by the reading. Acclamations, such as "alleluia" or "glory to you, O Lord," customarily precede and conclude the reading of the gospel. Finally, the hymn of the day serves as a congregational response to the entire liturgy of the word, as presented in the readings and the sermon. Through these responses, congregational song serves as an integral part of the proclamation of the word.

SILENCE

There is something to be said for silence. The liturgy of readings and responses, of solo voices and communal voices, can come across as words, words, words—one thing after another, with no time or space to absorb, to think, to pray. Recently I attended a conference at a college connected with a monastic community. The conference ran at a hectic pace, but time was allowed for participants to join the community in prayer. The monks were very deliberate in the pace of reading scripture, especially in reading the psalms responsively. The first time the conference members joined in the reading, they were always several "beats" ahead of the monks in speaking. It took several prayer times over a couple of days to appreciate a slower rhythm of speech and longer moments of silence. Once I made that adjustment I didn't want to return to the earlier pattern. Both scripture and prayer were fuller and richer for the time that silence allowed.

SERVING THE WORD

It is important to remember that the liturgy of the word serves the word. The reading of scripture is an event, it brings the written word of God alive in the ears and hearts of the people who are present. The sermon directs and invites us into a daily living with God's word. The community that has experienced God's presence and heard God's promises entrusts the concerns of the community to God in prayer. Hymn and prayer, creed and confession, speech and silence are all part of a pattern that serves Christ, in whom we meet God's grace, weekly and over a lifetime.

QUESTIONS FOR REFLECTION

What words in worship do you remember? What words confuse you? What words comfort you?

What difference does it make to think of this part of the service as the word *of* God and not words *about* God?

What problems or delights do you have with the Sunday readings? the sermon?

How do you share in the proclamation of the word?

CHAPTER FOUR

Bath

Even before her birth, her parents knew there was something wrong. At the time of birth the "something" wrong was found to be even worse than expected. Severe congenital birth defects meant a life measured in days, perhaps a few weeks. Her parents brought her home to die.

Her parents also brought her to church for baptism. They did not want an emergency baptism; their baby was not going to die "any minute." They wanted the full rite of the church: water and word (*all* the words), promises and prayers, the laying on of hands and anointing with oil, the lighting of a candle, and the welcome of the community. They wanted all the power and strength of God's promise declared and claimed in the face of what they knew was to come.

In my years as a pastor I had come to understand something of the connection between baptism and death. I had never presided at a funeral without thinking of baptism. The burial service begins with the reminder that "when we were baptized in Christ Jesus, we were baptized into his death" and the promise that "if we have been united with him in a death like his, we shall certainly be united with him in a resurrection like his" (*LBW*, Burial of the Dead; Rom. 6:3, 5). But never before had I thought so clearly of death at the time of a baptism. This baby's parents, in the face of their child's certain death, had presented her for baptism so that she might be freed from the power of sin and be raised up to a new life. In Christian love they brought her to the church to die, so that she might live.

Therefore we have been buried with [Christ] by baptism into death, so that, just as Christ was raised from the dead by the glory of the Father, so we too might walk in newness of life.

———

ROMANS 6:4

ஃ LOVE MADE VISIBLE

Not everyone thinks of baptism in such life and death terms. For some it is a rite of passage for infants, the church's way to mark a birth and get the child off to a good start. For others it is an initiation ceremony, the way you join the church at whatever age. For still others it is basically an option, a public way to say that God is important in my life. For some it is a kind of "fire insurance," a protection against eternal damnation. Some people present themselves or their children for baptism to please someone else—a spouse, parent or grandparent, even the community. Many view baptism as a private or, at the most, family event. While each of these views may hold elements of truth, the church claims that baptism is more.

Lutherans, along with many other Christians, believe that God comes to us not only in the word, but in the sacraments—those acts commanded by Christ in which an earthly element (water, bread, wine) is connected with God's word of promise to give God's grace. In Jesus Christ God showed us the fullness of divine love. Through the scriptures and their proclamation God continues to show this love. But words aren't always enough. They can be all too easily dismissed, especially when spoken in church, as being only about past people and events, or not being "for me." The sacraments are sometimes described as God's love made visible. When God's word of love and forgiveness comes with the feel of water on my head or the taste of bread and wine in my mouth, I can be sure that what the word promises is indeed "for me" in this place and time.

The exact number of sacraments differs from one Christian body to another. Lutherans have traditionally spoken of two, baptism and communion (*The Use of the Means of Grace*, principle 1). We understand both to have been commanded by Christ. Jesus told his disciples to "Go . . . and make disciples . . . , baptizing them in the name of the Father and of the Son and of the Holy Spirit" (Matt. 28:19). In offering his body and blood in the bread and wine of the first Lord's supper Jesus commanded the disciples to "Do this in remembrance of me" (Luke 22:19). In both, the earthly elements of water, bread, and wine are joined with God's word of promise to give us faith, forgiveness of sins, and new life.

℘ BELONGING

No one is born a Christian. We become Christians through becoming part of the Christian community. Baptism is the act by which God calls us into that community—giving us new birth, adopting us as children, and making us members of the church. These are all scriptural images. The image of new birth appears in the Gospel of John where Jesus tells Nicodemus, "no one can enter the kingdom of God without being born of water and Spirit" (John 3:5). Through baptism we become new creatures, enabled to turn our backs on our old selves and to turn toward new life in Christ.

Paul wrote to the Galatians that "God sent his Son . . . so that we might receive adoption as children" (Gal. 4:4-5). My husband and I are adoptive parents. We know the struggle and the joy of creating a family through adoption rather than birth. We knew from the beginning that our daughter was not our possession, no matter what we went through to "have" her. And so once she came to be with us we turned right around and placed her for another kind of adoption— we presented her for baptism. In that act she became God's child and a member of still another family, the church.

Baptism has been called "the womb of the church," giving birth to Christ's body in the world. In the water of baptism the Holy Spirit creates the church, making *many* persons *one* body. "For," says Paul, "in the one Spirit we were all baptized into one body" (1 Cor. 12:13). No matter what the age of the baptized, baptism is the act of entrance into the church universal and also into a particular congregation.

Baptism is a family event, but the family is the church family, not just the immediate family of the one being baptized. The members of the congregation, on behalf of the whole church, welcome the newly baptized into the Lord's family. That is why baptism takes place within communal worship. Even in cases of emergency, effort is made to gather members of the church family. Because baptism creates the community of faith, it needs to take place within and be shared with that community.

Baptism is a sacrament of belonging, belonging to God and to the church. It is for persons of all ages—infants and young children, older children and adults. We need to pay much more attention to unbaptized adults who come wondering and eager for God's grace in their lives. We also need to take seriously lifelong teaching and nurturing in the faith, that the baptized may be continually renewed in the meaning of baptism.

⁂ DYING AND RISING

Jesus' great commission is a major source of the church's understanding of baptism. "Go therefore and make disciples of all nations, baptizing them in the name of the Father and of the Son and of the Holy Spirit, and teaching them to obey everything that I have commanded you. And remember, I am with you always, to the end of the age" (Matt. 28:19-20). Other scripture passages are also part of the tradition, including Jesus' own baptism by John and the "baptism" of Jesus' death on the cross.

One of the major themes present in all these sources is our baptismal union with Jesus Christ. All the baptized stand with Jesus in the Jordan River, receiving the gift of the Spirit and being named as God's beloved children. We are especially joined with Jesus in his death and resurrection. Twice in the New Testament (Luke 12:50; Mark 10:38), Jesus speaks of his baptism not in terms of the Jordan event but of his impending death. Paul asserts that it is that death and God's act of resurrection to which we are joined in baptism: "when you were buried with him in baptism, you were also raised with him through faith in the power of God, who raised him from the dead" (Col. 2:12).

Perhaps the most powerful thing that can be said about baptism is that in it we experience in advance our own death and resurrection. We have faced the worst—the last great enemy, death—and have already claimed the promise of eternal life. God has done this once-for-all in Christ and has promised the same to us. This promise depends on God, not on us, and God does not lie.

A FRESH START

Baptism is a bath, a washing, an obvious natural sign of cleansing. Many religions have practiced ritual washing as a sign of spiritual cleansing. Water, after all, does make one clean. The baptismal service speaks of being liberated from sin and death, of cleansing and rebirth, of the washing away of sin.

Although we are baptized once, we spend our lives living out our baptism. Martin Luther described believers as being at the same time saints and sinners. We experience bondage to sin from which we cannot free ourselves even while we have been freed from sin and death. For Luther, the remembrance that he was baptized was the only way to claim God's promise of Christ for daily living. In his moments of deepest despair, Luther insisted, "There is no greater comfort on earth than baptism. . . . I am baptized, and through my baptism God, who cannot lie, has bound himself in a covenant with me" (Luther 1960).

There are many ways to join with Luther in remembering our baptisms. The confession of sin and receiving of forgiveness, whether in Sunday worship or in a private setting, is a return to the rejection of sin in baptism. Making the sign of the cross, a sign by which the baptized are marked, recalls our union with Christ's death and resurrection. Confessing the Apostles' Creed is a confession of baptismal faith. Daily prayer and scripture reading encourage us in daily dying and rising. Because of Jesus' death and resurrection and our own, in baptism, we are never trapped or stuck with what has been. God's promise makes a fresh start possible for us daily. With Luther we find comfort in God's unfailing promise, despite the mistakes and failings of daily life at work, in our homes, and in our communities. Over a lifetime, the remembering of baptism can transform the loss of a job, the experience of aging, and all moments of fear of the unknown into times of trust in the God who made and loves us.

℘ THE LITURGY OF THE BATH

Increasingly many Christians are seeking to celebrate baptism in such a way that its meaning and power in the lives of individual believers as well as the faith community shines forth. This celebration begins even before the liturgy of baptism with an emphasis on instruction that nurtures the faith. When infants and young children are baptized their parents and sponsors receive instruction. Older children and adult candidates themselves are invited into a period of instruction and formation called the *catechumenate*. In all cases, life-long learning enriches the baptized with renewed appreciation for the wonderful gifts given in baptism.

The celebration of baptism in Sunday worship not only acknowledges the presence of the welcoming community, but provides an opportunity for those who are gathered to remember and renew their own baptisms. The designation of great festivals—the Vigil of Easter, Pentecost, All Saints Day, and the Baptism of Our Lord—as occasions for baptism integrates the sacrament into the church year in a way that enriches the understanding of both. The Vigil of Easter is an ancient and especially appropriate time for baptism, helping Christians remember their burial and resurrection with Christ.

The cleansing and life-giving themes of baptism as well as its dying and rising action are heightened with a generous use of water and with large fonts, flowing water, and pools big enough for immersion. God, of course, can work through any amount of water and any size font. Baptism, however, is worth a practice that symbolizes God's power over sin and death. A moistened finger on the forehead looks more like dry cleaning than the washing away of sin. A sprinkle of water does little to convey that water can kill as well as bring life. At the very least, the use of the prayer of thanksgiving over the water, with its mighty biblical images, and the pouring of the baptismal water so that it can be seen and heard (even felt, by some) do better justice to the full meaning of baptism.

There are other signs that proclaim the meanings of baptism in all their richness. They include the laying on of hands and prayer for the coming of the Holy Spirit, the making of the sign of the cross, anointing with oil, clothing with a baptismal garment, and presenting a lighted candle. All of these actions are connected with scriptural images that proclaim the gifts given by the promise of God.

There is much discussion these days about the language of baptism, in particular the naming of the triune God. Baptism "in the name of the Father and of the Son and of the Holy Spirit" is what Jesus commanded in Matthew 28. There are those who find the words sexist— implying, if not insisting, that God is male. There are Christian traditions which baptize only "in the name of Jesus Christ." While baptism in the name of Father, Son, and Holy Spirit is the historic and ecumenically-received name, such baptism means much more than a recited formula. The "name" is a summary of and a teaching about the triune God, who created all that is, who is known to us in the crucified and risen Jesus, and who comes to us in the Spirit. Baptism in the name of the triune God is baptism that is accompanied, not by magic words, but by trinitarian life and teaching. It is that teaching that keeps the balance between the faith of the historic church and the honest concerns of our present day and time.

℘ COMPANIONS IN BAPTISMAL LIFE

If, along with Martin Luther, we understand baptism to be a lifelong covenant relationship of faith, then it is more than we can manage on our own. And we don't have to. Baptismal sponsors, sometimes called "godparents," guide and accompany us on this journey. It is not just infants who need sponsors. Adults also benefit from faith mentors who join them in prayer and mutual learning. Sponsors help to integrate the baptized, of whatever age, into the life and mission of the community of faith. While sponsors are often chosen from among the family or friends of the baptized, congregations are also encouraged to select congregational sponsors who take on the task of personifying the role of the community in supporting the baptismal life.

If it "takes a village to raise a child," then it can also be said that it takes a congregation to bring that child to faith. Many congregations understand their entire parish education program to be an integral part of baptismal ministry. God does not bring us to faith alone and does not ask us to grow by ourselves. Baptism is for the sake of life in Christ and in the body of Christ, the church.

Baptism is the sacrament that creates the church; communion is the sacrament that sustains it. We are baptized once, but God renews the same promise of faith, forgiveness, and new life each time we receive the gift of Jesus in bread and wine. We never know how long the baptismal life may be—hours, days, months, years—but we can trust God's promise to be with us.

We claim that promise as we continue in the covenant God made with us in baptism—by living among God's faithful people, by hearing the word and sharing the Lord's supper, by proclaiming the good news of God in Christ through word and deed, by serving all people, following the example of Jesus, and by striving for justice and peace in all the world (adapted from *LBW,* Affirmation of Baptism).

℘ QUESTIONS FOR REFLECTION/DISCUSSION

What do you know/remember about your own baptism?

What do you remember about the last baptism you witnessed? What was your role (parent, sponsor, the baptized, congregation member)? Do you think that made a difference in what you remember?

What do you like about the way your congregation celebrates baptism? What bothers you?

At this time in your life, what images of baptism (forgiveness of sin, adoption into God's family, union with Jesus Christ, new birth, the gift of the Holy Spirit, etc.) speak to you most directly? Why?

CHAPTER FIVE

Meal

My mother was a wonderful cook. She understood the importance of food for life, paying attention to diet and nutrition. Without food human beings die. She also understood the importance of food for community. All those things associated with growing, preparing, and eating food speak of love, comfort, and companionship. It became something of a joke among my college friends that my mother would encourage even the most casual of guests to "have just a bite" and then produce, seemingly without effort, a five-course meal.

> For as often as you eat this bread and drink the cup, you proclaim the Lord's death until he comes.
>
> 1 CORINTHIANS 11:26

GOD'S TABLE

My mother's way with food and hospitality had a profound impact on my image of God. God invites us again and again to a feast of love. In the very beginning God created a garden in Eden with green plants and fruit trees to provide food. The first paradise was a place of plenty. The exodus from slavery in Egypt was marked with a feast of roasted lamb and unleavened bread. Even in the wilderness God made sure there was water, manna, and meat for a wandering people. The psalms are full of images of being fed.

> The LORD is my shepherd, I shall not want.
>   He makes me lie down in green pastures;
> he leads me beside still waters . . .
> You prepare a table before me . . .
>   my cup overflows.
>
>   (Ps. 23:1-2, 5)

"Wisdom has set her table," says Proverbs, and "has sent out her servant girls" calling "Come, eat of my bread and drink of the wine I have mixed" (Prov. 9:2-3, 5). One of the prophets issues God's invitation to "come to the waters . . . come . . . eat" (Isa. 55:1), and sees the future with God in terms of "a feast of rich food, a feast of well-aged wines" (Isa. 25:6).

Jesus came eating and drinking, often with sinners. He changed water into wine and made a meal for 5,000 out of five loaves of bread and two fish. He told a story about a prodigal son who was welcomed home with a wonderful feast, and another about a marriage feast to which even street people were invited. It's not surprising then, that God would choose to come to us in a meal.

℘ THE LORD'S SUPPER

On the night before he died Jesus ate a meal with his disciples. It was a Jewish meal, the Passover feast, kept to celebrate God's gift of liberation. It was a meal that already included bread and wine, thanksgiving and sharing, but Jesus transformed it into a new meal in which Jesus' own body and blood became the food. This is the meal we share in our Sunday gathering.

The pattern of our meal comes from the scriptural accounts of that first Lord's supper (Matt. 26:26-29; Mark 14:22-25; Luke 22:15-20) and Paul's teaching to the Corinthians.

> For I received from the Lord what I also handed on to you, that the Lord Jesus on the night when he was betrayed took a loaf of bread, and when he had given thanks, he broke it and said, "This is my body that is for you. Do this in remembrance of me." In the same way he took the cup also, after supper, saying, "This cup is the new covenant in my blood. Do this, as often as you drink it, in remembrance of me." For as often as you eat this bread and drink the cup, you proclaim the Lord's death until he comes (1 Cor. 11:23-26).

Paul reminds us that the meal is a proclamation. It is a visible word. Using the real stuff of bread and wine God conveys the presence of the crucified and risen Christ. The words Christ spoke on the night of his betrayal are spoken so everyone present can see and hear what this meal really is and who is the true host. Jesus Christ is truly present in this meal, although the "how" of that remains a mystery. It is, finally, enough that we hear God's word of promise to be with us and that we trust that promise.

✌ FOR YOU

Communion is more than a memory or a reenactment of a past event. It is a living event in which Christ's body and blood are given and shed "for you." Although communion takes place within the gathered community, it is also personal and direct. Through the gift of Christ's body and blood God nourishes our faith, forgives our sins, and calls us to lives of service and witness. We need this gift often. We need not only to hear God's word but to see, taste, touch, and smell it. Many Christian churches, including a steadily increasing number of Lutheran churches, celebrate communion every Sunday and festival.

The Lord's supper is for the baptized, all who are gathered and who are members of the body of Christ. It is given as a gift, given to faith by and for participation in the community of faith. Jesus gave no command regarding the age at which people should be baptized or first receive communion. The Lord's invitation to communion is presented through the church. Congregations take their role seriously, establishing practices of invitation, education, and reception of communion. They seek to balance Christ's command to "do this," the promise of his presence, our human need, and good order in the church.

My own first communion took place after I was confirmed. That was the established practice of my congregation, and I don't regret the way in which I was taught the power and meaning of the sacrament. But my confirmation congregation did not seem to know how to invite and teach those who didn't fit the accepted pattern. I remember a Christmas Eve candlelight communion service in the days when only those who communed went forward to the altar rail. Two young children (perhaps 4 and 6 years old) came forward for communion, unaccompanied by any adult. They were well behaved, clearly imitating what others were doing. The pastors gave bread and wine and shared God's "for you" with each communicant, but then bypassed the two children without a word.

At the time, it never occurred to me that children might commune. I was, however, haunted by the missed opportunity to speak Christ in some way to and for them. The communion practices of Lutheran congregations have always emphasized trust in God's promise that Jesus is for you and that this gift is for the forgiveness of sins. Lutherans have valued lifelong teaching and mutual conversation about communion, and many congregations are now inviting younger children and even infants to receive the sacrament.

✥ FOR OTHERS

Communion in many congregations is not just for members of those congregations. All baptized persons are welcome, even visitors. Often there will be a brief statement, written or spoken, explaining something of how the congregation understands Christ to be truly present in communion. Such a statement allows visitors to decide whether or not to accept the invitation. It may be that someone who has not been baptized receives communion. That would not be cause for shame either on the part of that person or of the one giving communion. We can rejoice that Christ comes to everyone and that all are invited to learn about the faith of the church, be baptized, and become regular communicants.

The Lord's supper is a communal meal, to be shared by the community of faith. Weekly communion is one way in which members of the community are able to share in the family meal. But what about those who are unable to attend church because they are sick, homebound, or imprisoned? In the early days of the church provision was made for bread and wine to be taken to the absent as an extension of Sunday worship. Many congregations have continued that practice, and many pastors regularly share word and sacrament in homes and hospitals and other institutions. Including others from the congregation in those celebrations strengthens the community.

✺ THE LITURGY OF THE MEAL

Just as there is a pattern to the proclamation of the word, there is a pattern to the celebration of the meal. It is the same fourfold pattern that is to be found in the words repeated over the bread and wine—Jesus took bread, gave thanks, broke it, and gave it.

We receive bread and wine, along with money and other gifts, in what we call the offering. In the early church, the Lord's supper stretched over a full meal with the breaking of the bread at the beginning and the sharing of the cup at the end. For a variety of reasons this became condensed into a simple meal that could be eaten by many people at once. But people still brought food to be shared and money to give to those in need. These gifts, along with the bread and wine for communion, were brought to the altar together. When we receive an offering at the beginning of the communion meal we are reminded that receiving Christ means being mindful of others.

When Jesus gave thanks over the bread and cup he was following Jewish tradition, offering a prayer of blessing that included thanks and praise for the presence and action of God in all the events of life. The words of Jesus recorded in scripture were likely only a part of that prayer. We call those the words of institution, words by which Jesus commanded us to keep the feast. The early church adopted a similar pattern of prayer and thanksgiving—offered by one person, called by Justin Martyr the presider, the same person who preached. This is the table grace of the community, giving thanks and praise for what God has done in the past and for the gift of Christ in the bread and wine. The whole congregation responds, singing out "their assent, saying the 'Amen'" (from the Apology of Justin Martyr).

The next thing Jesus did was to break the bread, a practical matter surely if the bread was to be shared among many. Early Christians found significance in the idea of one loaf, broken and shared. It was a sign for them of the unity to be found in Christ. Paul reminded the Corinthians, "Because there is one bread, we who are many are one body, for we all partake of the one bread" (1 Cor. 10:17). We are called to take this same truth seriously in our own lives; unity in Christ triumphs over all human differences—of culture, class, nation, and gender.

Jesus' giving of the bread and cup to his disciples is what we do in distributing communion. There are many ways to share the bread and wine, although some (such as one loaf and one cup) seem to speak more clearly of the unity of the sacrament. There are and will probably continue to be disagreements about the use of bread or wafers, wine or grape juice, kneeling or standing, individual glasses or common cup, music or silence. Whatever decisions about these things are made in a given congregation, they should reflect as best as possible the unity of the body of Christ and the dignity of those who commune. Each communicant needs to hear the promise of Christ: "The body of Christ given for you . . . the blood of Christ shed for you."

✥ A CELEBRATION OF THE CHURCH

Despite differences between congregations in the celebration of communion, the sacrament is not the possession of a congregation, but of Christ, who gives it through the church. Christ is both the host and the meal. The presence of an ordained minister as presider is not to act out the role of Jesus, as though the liturgy of the meal is a stage play, but to serve the unity of the church. Presiding is not something one person does while others watch, it is one leadership role among several. Ordained ministers have been specially trained and called to preach the gospel and administer the sacraments—the means by which God gives faith, forgiveness of sins, and new life.

The Lord's supper is a meal. It reminds us that God cares for us in a very basic way, by providing the food which sustains our bodies. But this meal sustains more than our physical bodies. It is a meal for forgiveness of sin and eternal life; it sustains our spirits. In the bread we are given the very being of Christ. In the cup Christ's life is poured out in blood. In, with, and under bread and wine comes the incredible gift of God's grace.

This meal is a *eucharist*, an occasion of thanksgiving for creation and for what God has done in Jesus Christ. It is a *liturgy*, a public action carried out by a community of people. It is a *service*, reminding us of God's astonishing service to us and our calling to respond in service to our neighbor. It is a *mass* that sends us out in mission.

This meal is a *communion* that, through God's Spirit, forms believers of all times and places throughout the world into one body. It is a foretaste of the feast to come when we will be united in our singing and praying and eating with the whole company of heaven.

> Let the vineyards be fruitful, Lord,
>   and fill to the brim our cup of blessing.
> Gather a harvest from the seeds that were sown,
>   that we may be fed with the bread of life.
> Gather the hopes and dreams of all;
>   unite them with the prayers we offer.
> Grace our table with your presence,
>   and give us a foretaste of the feast to come
>   (*LBW*, Holy Communion).

✒ QUESTIONS FOR REFLECTION

What memories do you have of special foods or meals?

What was your first experience of communion? How has your experience changed over time?

When have you had a clear sense of God's gifts being "for you?" When have you felt distanced from God?

What connections do you see between communion and your daily life?

CHAPTER SIX

Sending

There is a church in central Minnesota with somewhat unusual architecture. The *narthex*, the gathering place, is located in what many would call the front of the church. When people gather for worship, large sliding doors stand open between the narthex and the worship space, which people enter by walking around and past the altar. As they take their seats they face the way from which they came. At the beginning of the liturgy the doors are closed, focusing attention on the places of word and sacrament. During the final hymn the doors are opened again. In this building there is no mistaking the intention of the final words of the liturgy, "Go in peace. Serve the Lord." Service to God is service in the world. "Thanks be to God," responds the congregation, looking beyond pulpit and altar to the parking lot, neighborhood, and community beyond.

What we call the
beginning is often
the end.
And to make an end is
to make a beginning.
The end is where we
start from.

T. S. ELIOT

ENDINGS AND BEGINNINGS

The gathering and the sending movements of worship share a simplicity of shape and purpose. The music, words, and prayer of gathering bring us together in all our diversity and shape us into a community. They set the tone for what is to come by preparing us to hear the word, remember baptism, and share the meal. While the gathering rite may be as short and simple as a greeting and prayer or enriched with procession and hymn, it does not overshadow what is to come.

In the same way the sending rite does not unnecessarily stretch out what has already happened. Through word and sacrament the community has been strengthened and is ready to be sent into the mission field that is the world. There is no need for delay; there is great wisdom in bringing things quickly to a close. "Go" is not a suggestion but a command. Like a football team breaking the huddle, no one wants to be called for delaying the game.

Both the gathering and the sending come from God. God calls the church into being and sends the church into the world. We are greeted in "the grace of our Lord Jesus Christ, the love of God, and the communion of the Holy Spirit" (*LBW* and *With One Voice*, Holy Communion). In worship we meet the living Christ, not just the memory of one who lived, died, and was raised nearly two thousand years ago. As we gather in God's presence we must be open to the impact of that real presence.

We are sent on our way, not with a vote for adjournment as if the assembly was a business meeting, but with words of blessing and peace. "The Lord bless you and keep you. The Lord make his face shine on you and be gracious to you. The Lord look upon you with favor and give you peace" (*LBW*, Holy Communion). The God of grace and peace, the living God, promises to go with us into the times and places of our daily lives.

℘ BLESSING

Blessing is a powerful act, a sign of God's gracious care in daily life. The words of blessing are not an expressed hope, a request, or a prayer. We do not ask the Lord to bless us and be gracious to us. They are words of faith and fact. They are not just wishful thinking, but true signs of

God's presence and power. God is with us. God looks upon us with favor and gives us peace.

The God we come to know in Jesus Christ, in word and sacrament, is a God who is at work in the world. Sometimes God works through dramatic interventions in history: freedom from slavery in Egypt, coming to live among us in Jesus. But God also works among us in the day-to-day blessings of life and health, home and family, work and leisure, planting and harvesting—all signs of God's steadfast faithfulness.

When we leave worship with God's blessing ringing in our ears we carry with us the assurance of the presence of God in all our comings and goings. It is no accident that the English "good-bye," like the French "adieu" or the Spanish "adios," is a fervent wish that "God be with you."

SUNDAY INTO MONDAY

It is not God alone who accompanies us from Sunday into our Monday worlds. Those who have been gathered in God's name and shaped into a community of faith continue to walk with one another. Throughout the week the members of the community stay in touch with one another through prayer, with and for each other, in mutual conversation and consolation, in gatherings for study, action, and service. Such activities flow out of Sunday worship and look forward to the next Sunday's gathering.

God's word leads us into lives of prayer and proclamation. It is out of the word and promise of God that we can pray for one another and for the needs of the world. In prayer we name, with all the integrity we can muster, the honesty of both scripture and preaching, the real pains and struggles of our world. We name names and sins, needs and hopes. In our praying we remember that we are God's first answer to our own prayers. Prayer is not just spoken, but lived. Christians are called by God to be workers in the kingdom, a presence of faith, hope, and love.

God's word is a word to be shared. Although we tend to think of the pastor as the preacher—the one who bears responsibility for proclaiming the gospel in public worship—all the baptized share that responsibility. Lutherans have a reputation for not being very good at sharing their faith. A Lutheran bishop tells of how he and his wife agreed to be neighborhood captains for an American Cancer Society fund drive. They went door to door, sharing their understanding of the work and continuing needs of the society. When they returned home they realized that this was the first time they had talked to many of their neighbors about something so important. Why, they wondered, had it not been conversation about faith or an invitation to church?

Even in North America, for all that we tend to think of ourselves as people of faith, there are many in every community who have not heard the good news of what God has done in Jesus Christ or who do not think that such good news is for them. How are they to hear without someone inviting them? And when they come will they have a sense that it is *good* news, that lives are changed in an encounter with Jesus Christ? Jesus commanded his followers to make disciples of all nations, and that includes the people next door.

℅ CHRISTIAN VOCATION

In my first year as a pastor, a ninth grade confirmation student asked me, "What do you do during the rest of the week? Do you have a job or something?" I laughed (and have gotten more than a few laughs myself in telling the story), but I have to admit I was a bit offended by the question. Didn't she have any sense at all that being a pastor was a full-time job—even more than full-time? Probably not! Although it wasn't part of her vocabulary or conscious intention, she was really asking a question about Christian vocation.

For many people "vocation" means job or occupation, usually that for which they get paid. Some Christians use the word to speak of a calling to religious life as priest, monk, or nun. Lutherans speak of Christian vocation as an expression of baptismal life. We have many vocations, many callings, for the relationships, work, citizenship, and activities of daily life are all included. God calls us to serve in the home and school and workplace, in our hobbies and leisure activities, as friends and neighbors and citizens. Martin Luther was particularly insistent that all vocations are to be honored as spheres of God's activity—the butcher, the father or mother changing diapers, and the pastor all serve God. No one—not even the pastor—spends twenty-four hours a day in church! But God has a claim on all twenty-four hours. We each have many vocations and live out those baptismal callings in the balance and the mix of home, work, and activity.

We are strengthened in our vocations when we cling to baptism and repeatedly affirm it. Every baptism celebrated in public worship is an occasion for the remembrance and renewal of our own baptisms. An occasion of baptism can be a wonderful opportunity for parents to talk with children, or for Sunday school teachers to talk with students about baptism and its meaning for daily life.

There is a rite for affirmation of baptism that is often used at confirmation, when young men and women who have come to identify more deeply with the community of faith participate more fully in the church's mission. When new members join a congregation or when those who have been absent seek restoration of membership, affirmation of baptism is a powerful statement about the grounding of Christian identity.

What could be even more powerful is the repeated affirmation of baptism at times of change in life. Becoming parents or grandparents, choosing, changing, or retiring from an occupation, moving away from home, being diagnosed with a chronic illness, the ending of a relationship or of a first year of mourning, release from prison, the blending of a family through a new marriage, and release from abuse or addiction are all life changes that can be placed within the context of Christian vocation through affirming baptism.

HUNGER FOR JUSTICE

Part of our baptismal calling is to work for peace and justice in all the world. Every Lord's supper reminds us that food is God's good gift, necessary for life. A college student told me that he hated the practice of "continuous communion" where those who distribute the bread and wine stand in one place and the communicants come to them in a continuous procession. His reason? "It makes me feel like I'm standing in the cafeteria line." This student clearly cherished communion and seemed to think that it would somehow be denigrated by association with the school food service. But, in fact, the reverse is what can happen. Communion blesses all food and restores to our eating a sense of gift. A continuous procession may, in fact, be a helpful reminder that we are a people on the move, bringing to the world what we have shared.

Every meal also reminds us that many in our world go hungry, lacking even the smallest amounts necessary for life. A bite of bread and a sip of wine may not seem like much to those who have plenty to eat, but as God's gift to us this food strengthens us not only to share but to pray and work for enough food for all. Communion is a "foretaste of the feast to come," not only in the sense of the heavenly banquet, but also of God's intention that God's gifts be shared.

It is not just those who are hungry who are of concern to God and whom we remember in this meal. When we share the peace of God with one another, it is not just a casual "hello," but a heartfelt prayer. God's intention for peace goes beyond the gathering to the whole world. Those who wish peace to and for one another are also called to find ways to work for peace in their homes, communities, nations, and the world.

Communion is more than food; it is also the gift of faith, of forgiveness, and of salvation, which is wholeness, health, peace, and eternal life. This is what God intends for the universe that God created and loves. This is the justice for which God calls us to witness and to work. Martin Luther said it well:

> When you have partaken of this sacrament, therefore, or desire to partake of it, you must in turn share the misfortunes of the fellowship . . . Here your heart must go out in love and learn that this is a sacrament of love. As love and support are given to you, you in turn must render love and support to Christ in his needy ones. You must feel with sorrow all the dishonor done to Christ in his holy Word, all the misery of Christendom, all the unjust suffering of the innocent, with which the world is

everywhere filled to overflowing. You must fight, work, pray, and—if you cannot do more—have heartfelt sympathy (Luther 1989).

❧ GATHERED AND SENT

Our worship begins and ends with God. God calls us from the world, and shapes and sustains us as a community of faith by the living presence of Jesus Christ in word and sacrament. God sends us back into the world to be signs of that presence not only for ourselves but for all. It is in this world that we spend our time, but never alone. God is with us.

> God is here! As we your people meet to offer praise and prayer,
> may we find in fuller measure what it is in Christ we share.
> Here, as in the world around us, all our varied skills and arts
> wait the coming of the Spirit into open minds and hearts.
>
> Here are symbols to remind us of the lifelong need of grace;
> here are table, font, and pulpit; here the cross has central place.
> Here in honesty of preaching, here in silence, as in speech,
> here, in newness and renewal, God the Spirit comes to each.
>
> Here our children find a welcome in the Shepherd's flock and fold;
> here as bread and wine are taken, Christ sustains us, as of old.
> Here the servants of the Servant seek in worship to explore
> what it means in daily living to believe and to adore.

(Fred Pratt Green, *With One Voice*, #719)

❧ QUESTIONS FOR REFLECTION/DISCUSSION

What are your vocations in the world? How does the church support you in your callings?

What have you felt so strongly about that you have had to share it with others? How is that like or different from what you feel about your faith?

How do you (or don't you) stay connected to the faith community between Sundays?

When have you experienced a strong connection between Sunday worship and daily life? When have you experienced the two as totally separate worlds?

Seasons and Principal Festivals of the Church Year

ADVENT is the first season in the church year. It is a period of four weeks before the celebration of Christmas. Advent draws attention toward the long-awaited birth of Jesus at Bethlehem, and to Christ's second coming in the future.

CHRISTMAS annually commemorates the birth of Christ. It is a festival season lasting twelve days, from December 25 until Epiphany on January 6.

EPIPHANY is a festival on January 6 marking the visit of wise men from the East to the newborn Christ. The season after Epiphany incorporates the festivals of the *Baptism of Our Lord* (first Sunday after Epiphany) and the *Transfiguration of Our Lord* (last Sunday after Epiphany). The *Sundays after the Epiphany* vary in number owing to the dating of Easter, which may be celebrated either in late March or sometime in April.

LENT is a period of forty days prior to the celebration of the Three Days. Beginning with *Ash Wednesday*, Lent also incorporates *Passion (Palm) Sunday* in its final week. Lent is one of the primary times to focus on baptismal preparation for those awaiting baptism, and for baptismal renewal of all Christians.

THE THREE DAYS start with the evening of Maundy Thursday and continue to the evening of Easter Day (Easter Evening). While it is the shortest of the church year seasons, these days proclaim the center of the Christian faith: that Christ died, rose again, and will bring us also from life to death. The Three Days include *Maundy Thursday, Good Friday, Easter Vigil, and Easter Day.*

EASTER is an entire season encompassing fifty days. It is a "week of weeks." *The Day of Pentecost* occurs on the fiftieth day, celebrating the sending of the Holy Spirit. The festival of the *Ascension of Our Lord* occurs on the fortieth day of the season.

THE SEASON AFTER PENTECOST incorporates half of the church year, and the days are numbered as *Sundays after Pentecost.* Though *Holy Trinity* (first Sunday after Pentecost) to *Christ the King* (last Sunday after Pentecost) is all one season, this time may be subdivided into Summer, Autumn, and November.

Acknowledgments

Contemporary Worship 2. Copyright © 1970 by Lutheran Church in America, Synod of Evangelical Lutheran Churches, The American Lutheran Church, The Evangelical Lutheran Church of Canada, and The Lutheran Church—Missouri Synod.

Eliot, T.S. "Little Gidding," in *Four Quartets.* Copyright © 1943 by T.S. Eliot and renewed 1971 by Esme Valerie Eliot. Reprinted by permission of Harcourt Brace & Company.

Green, Fred Pratt. "God Is Here," in *With One Voice.* Text copyright © 1979 Hope Publishing Co. Used by permission.

Heschel, Abraham Joshua. *The Sabbath.* New York: Farrar, Straus and Young, Inc., 1951. Originally published in Berthold Auerbach, *Poet and Merchant* (New York: H. Holt, 1877).

Luther, Martin. "The Large Catechism of Dr. Martin Luther," in *The Book of Concord.* Theodore G. Tappert, trans. and ed. Philadelphia: Fortress Press, 1959.

———. "The Holy and Blessed Sacrament of Baptism," in *Luther's Works*, Vol. 35. Trans. Jeremiah J. Schindel. Rev. E. Theodore Bachmann. Philadelphia: Fortress Press, 1960.

———. "The Blessed Sacrament of the Holy and True Body and Blood of Christ, and the Brotherhoods," in *Martin Luther's Basic Theological Writings.* Ed. Timothy F. Lull. Minneapolis: Fortress Press, 1989.

The Use of the Means of Grace: A Statement on the Practice of Word and Sacrament. Copyright © 1997 by Evangelical Lutheran Church in America.

Wengert, Timothy J., trans. *A Contemporary Translation of Luther's Small Catechism.* Minneapolis: Augsburg Fortress, 1994.